Published by:
CSA Cookbooks, Inc
37 Tremont Street
Cambridge, MA 02139
www.csacookbooks.com
617-868-5995

CSACOOKBOOKS
Custom Cookbooks for Local Farmers

WINTER FOODS

RECIPES AND COOKING TIPS FROM EVEN' STAR ORGANIC FARM

Featuring Over 50 Seasonally-Inspired Recipes Designed Especially For Your CSA Winter Subscription

The Even' Star Organic Farm Winter Cookbook

This cookbook was prepared by Julia Shanks and Brett Grohsgal of Even' Star Organic Farm to help our CSA customers enjoy the foods that we so love to plant, tend, and harvest. Our farm is certified organic. We are totally devoted to ethical land stewardship and to growing lovely flowers and outstandingly flavored foods. These hundred acres are located in St. Mary's County, Maryland: 48322 Far Cry Road, Lexington Park, MD 20653; (301) 866 1412.

We thank all of our customers for supporting local farms. You are the people that may let progressive American farms survive and maybe even thrive into the 21st century. You make possible our stewardship and environmental goals.

I dedicate this cookbook to the two wonderful Italian women who taught me to cook: my mother Roberta and my grandmother Tess. Kids need to learn from great traditional cooks, and for many kids no finer afternoon can be spent than a winter one when a loved adult is teaching how they learned to make a fine meal, many decades past. I treasure all that Roberta and Tess taught me.

I could not have created this cookbook without the incredible professional assistance of Julia Shanks (www.GrowCookEat.com). Julia's dedication to great foods, passion for fresh-from-the-earth flavors, and ability to effortlessly teach cooking to kitchen novices has contributed immeasurable to both her success and to our table.

We acknowledge that recipes are in the public domain once printed. We encourage you to use and share these recipes most freely. We ask nonetheless that you credit the source, Even' Star Organic Farm, when and if you copy or distribute any recipes from this cookbook.

Thank you!
Brett Grohsgal - Even' Star Organic Farm

TABLE OF CONTENTS

About this Book

Welcome to the Even' Star Organic Farm Winter Cookbook!

We have created this Orion Issue for our winter subscribers in the hope that it will ease your preparation of the many foods that we grow in the cold months. These superb greens and savory roots are not often found in supermarkets or in better cookbooks. The recipes come from our lifelong love of fine meals, from (Brett's) 18 years as a professional chef (yes, we did have a few normal jobs before we became a farmer), from Julia's 17 years as a chef and food professional. Brett's wife Christine and many of our CSA members have also contributed outstanding recipes. We name the winter issue after the Orion constellation. It shines strikingly right above our home and fields on many frigid and crystal-clear nights. Orion is a most welcome companion during the glorious winter farming season.

This volume has five sections:

Introduction
Our Winter Offerings
Storing your Produce for Optimal Freshness
Key Techniques and Definitions of Terms
The Recipes

We strongly suggest that you read the first four brief sections before you try any recipes. This is because the Introduction shows you the biases and assumptions that shape each recipe and even the crops that we choose to grow. Techniques are the essential verbs of cooking. The Food Descriptions are simplified reflections of my deep familiarity with each of these crops, and have further been refined by feedback from the chefs whose restaurants receive many of our foods. The single page of Abbreviations keeps extra words, space, and tedium to a bare minimum.

Introduction

We hold to the Italian prejudice in cooking that superb ingredients simply prepared are always better than mediocre ingredients prepared even with great skill and complicated recipes. Our heirloom vegetables, berries, and melons are testimony to this ethic. But we also urge the omnivores among you to buy safe, free-ranging meats from local farmers. These will complement the foods that our farm grows better than can any conveniently packaged but not necessarily safe, or organic, or free-range, meats or poultry from national supermarket chains. We urge you to know the farmer from whom you buy your meats, or to reconsider how much meat you are eating. This is the surest guarantor of wonderful flavors and superior safety. Your health, tummies, and palates will welcome the shift towards more local and less processed foods. We know this from personal experience: we can no longer digestively handle fast foods or many kinds of commercial, mass-marketed meats. And we remain appalled at the poor quality of globally-shipped fruits and vegetables.

Our second prejudice is that moderation in all things can be a rather nice path. Yes, we love wine, and aged bourbon, and chanterelle mushrooms, and a great steak. But we consider a meal a real meal only if it includes the salad course, be it of August heirloom tomatoes or of February frost-sweetened mesclun. We also are partial to carbohydrates as the superior fuel for hard-working bodies, though protein-heavy diets have without doubt slimmed many Americans. We hence often include suggestions for an appropriate starch to accompany our vegetables.

We also deeply distrust ostensibly scientific findings that any one food is bad for us. We remember that era when we were all told that margarine is healthier than butter, as well as the subsequent short-lived time when equally sincere researchers told us that olive oil is bad and soy oil is good. Our bias is that traditional cuisines tell us what is good for us more often than can researchers.

Our final prejudice was instilled in us by way, way too many years in restaurant kitchens. The right time needed for something to be perfectly cooked cannot be dictated by any cookbook or timer. Suggested cooking times are hence only crude approximations: thc most key phrase in the kitchen is "cook 'til done". If a recipe that we read says cook for 25 minutes at 350°F, we check the "doneness" at 18 minutes, at 22 minutes, at 25 minutes, and on and on. And we never assume that the thermostat temp is really accurate, nor that foods cook as fast or as evenly in the middle of the oven versus at the edges of the oven. Our eyes and experience are better gauges for every dish than anyone's printed words, including my own.

CHAPTER 1: Descriptions of Our Winter Offerings

The following covers most of the crops we grow every winter but ignores both warm-season crops and special rare items. These next are our staples, and you'll get an emailed list every week of what we have harvested for you. For the first few weeks we'll also strive to label your Ziplocs as to contents, so you can match up the lovely greens with the individual crop descriptions below.

Our farm grows some of the best salad and cooking greens you can find. This is because most of our greens are grown in the cold months--when the leaves are tender, and chilly nights sweeten the crop. Most of our cool-season vegetables are also really healthy: 80% of these are members of the Brassica family (i.e., the cold crops), rich in cancer-fighting anti-oxidants.

Winter farming in the Chesapeake region produces great flavors but is essentially a harvesting dance around ice, snow, and freeze. The winter weather also dramatically alters leaf colors. With real cold, arugula, collards, kales, and some of the mustards can have purple casts. After the most extreme freezes, a white or silvery sheen is also seen, especially on collards, kales, and tat soi. These are the "frost-bit" or "frost-kissed" phenomena and are marks of the highest quality. Sugars concentrate in these leaves and we invite you to directly compare these cold-raised greens with the stuff coming from warm farms far, far away.

All produce is washed 1-2 times. Excluding whole heads (crowns), baby turnips, baby rutabagas, and radishes, you don't get roots or long stems, just ready-for-use, zero-waste loose greens. The only items you need to wash once more are the root crops and those greens sold as whole heads (e.g. Michihili, Tat Soi, Pac Choi, and Maruba Santoh).

We advise that you store these in the refrigerator, in the same Ziploc into which we send them to you, but adding a paper towel and inverting the bag to absorb extra water. If you need extended shelf life, line a Tupperware with cloth or paper towels, place the greens on top, and cover with lid.

WINTER HARDY GREENS

ROBUST SALAD MIX AKA ITALIAN WILTING MIX

Larger leaves of our intense arugula mixed with milder greens such as tat soi, tenderleaf, Pac choi, et al. This is very good mixed with bland tomatoes or lettuces to perk up the latter. A favorite fall salad is this blend (coarsely chopped) and slices of really good apples like Staymans or Winesaps. Dress with olive oil, balsamic or sherry vinegar, and salt and pepper. Also makes a great salad with pear slices and goat cheese or even grated Gouda. Robust salad mix is also a blend we recommend for Caesar salads, for sandwiches, and for adding to soups, risotto dishes, and pastas (coarsely chopped) right before serving.

MESCLUN

A state-of-the-art blend of the smallest leaves: tenderleaf, tat soi, baby collards or kale, arugula, 2 kinds of Asian mustards, and 4 kinds of oak leaf and butter lettuces and/or rose petals when available. Ours is far more flavorful than old, lettuce-dominated mesclun from California or Mexico. Eat this mix pure, or blend it with lettuces. The best dressing to maximize flavor is just olive oil, lemon juice, salt and pepper (optionally, add raw onion and cilantro). Other really good dressings substitute high quality red wine, sherry, or balsamic vinegars for the lemon juice. Mesclun is fine on sandwiches and kids favor its small leaves, especially the more mild oval-shaped ones like baby collards, tat soi, and tenderleaf. Keeps about 3-6 days, well chilled.

ARUGULA

This is one of our most pungent greens, not to everyone's taste. Outstanding salad uses for arugula are with pears or apples, or mixed with romaine, sweet red peppers or boring out-of-season tomatoes. It is traditional and superb to use this in sandwiches paired with Brie, Camembert, chevre, prosciutto, turkey, ham, or roast beef. For those who can't handle the pungency raw, arugula is wonderful in garlic-enriched broth soups or briefly cooked with other greens.

STIR-FRY BLEND

This is the most popular of our cooking greens. We harvest and mix the greens that will give the best flavor balance, and the proportions and inclusions depend on how the different crops respond to that week's weather. Stir-fry blend can include curly or smooth kales, Georgia Butter or Champion collards, mizuna, 5 kinds of Asian or American mustards, turnip salad, tenderleaf, lamb's quarters (a wild amaranth), and/or English cress. Cook it only a minute or so—it's that tender. Great ways to prepare it include a) sauté with garlic and olive oil; b) stir-fry with sesame oil, ginger, and garlic; c) stir into a vegetable or chicken broth (or soup, for example, with capellini or tortellini) right after the broth is fully seasoned and has reached a simmer; d) blanch until wilted in boiling salted water; or e) substitute for spinach in lasagna, quiche, or spanokopita. Regardless of how you cook this blend, it will perk up any meal or dish.

The most common way we cook greens is to sauté them following blanching/shocking. The shocking may be omitted if the initial blanching is immediately followed by the sauté. Pre-wilting by blanching or steaming reduces the wateriness of the final dish and lets the other ingredients stay crisp. There are two basic approaches, Italian and Chinese, and each may be modified in countless ways. All involve coarsely chopping the greens and salting and peppering to taste, so these are implied but not spelled out in the following.

COLLARDS

Properly grown and harvested, collards are superbly mild, sweet and tender. "Properly" means winter, when our collards will outshine spinach for delicate flavor. Our mixed collards are two old-time varieties grown for taste, plus the milder and most tender Champion collards. The old-fashioned varieties have oval leaves with smooth margins. Champion has lobed leaves and looks much like smooth kale. Our collards are wonderful cooked only 30 to 45 seconds in any of the sauté or soup approaches that will follow.

CURLY AND SMOOTH KALES

Nicely raised kales are like properly managed collards: mild, tender, and delicate. We harvest ours often to keep any of the leaves from getting old or tough, so they need only 30-90 seconds of cooking. Smooth kale is sweet and really tender. Curly kale has more body and more chew, especially by February, and so at that point it begins to be superior for hearty soups or (for our restaurants) to add plate height to other sautéed greens.

WHOLE-CROWN TAT SOI

A crown is a whole plant that grew low to the ground and was cut from its roots, as per a head of Romaine. Whole crowns here and in the following descriptions give you more shelf life and versatility, but we do advise washing them once more. Tat soi is really versatile: mild, tender, and nice in salads, sandwiches, steamed, in soups, sautéed, whatever! Keep the midrib and petiole (the white stem-like thing) on for its sweet succulence. The whole crown is even grill-able.

WHOLE-CROWN MARUBA SANTOH

Really, really mild, these palest green heads look like lettuce. Maruba Santoh is actually a Japanese heirloom related to the Napa cabbages.

Use in sandwiches, salads, or sauté only 30 seconds or so whole, with ginger and garlic, soy sauce and butter. Outstanding for its delicacy.

WHOLE-CROWN PAC CHOI

These look like tat soi but are more pungent (mustardy) in flavor. They add a nice bite to sandwiches and salads, and they totally tone down when cooked. As versatile as tat soi and Maruba Santoh.

CHINESE THICK-STEM MUSTARD

A truly great heirloom. Thick midrib, sweetness, tender juicy bite, and sturdiness when cooked make this our personal favorite. The most balanced and the least pungent of any of the classical mustards we grow. Can be added to salads, sautéed, steamed, added late to soups, or used in hearty sandwiches. It's even grill-able.

AMERICAN CURLY MUSTARD

Lovely frilled leaves belie the intense mustardy bite of this one. Brief cooking greatly reduces the pungency. This is excellent in vegetarian bean dishes or with pork or beef. Eat raw only if you are a lover of wasabi, horseradish, or cress.

MIXED MUSTARDS

The above two, mixed with the heirloom Osaka Purple Mustard. Cook as per American Curly.

ENGLISH CRESS (AKA FIELD CRESS)

Whole crowns, so wash once more. Robust and better than most watercress. Use raw as per watercress, added to soups late, or mixed with other greens in sauté dishes

MICHIHILI

A mild Chinese cabbage with open heads. Sweet, succulent, and delicate for brief sauté; excellent cooked whole as per Maruba Santoh. Bristly feel disappears with cooking.

Root Vegetables

WHITE TURNIPS, GOLD TURNIPS, AND PURPLE-TOP TURNIPS

Tender and outstanding, roasted, braised, or simmered. Very nice raw, sliced 1/16"– 1/8" thin, then dipped into soy sauce or a vegetable dip. Peeling optional. Tops (greens) may be washed once more and sautéed or braised as per any of our cooking greens. Tops are supposedly higher in calcium and potassium than other cooking greens.

COLETTO VIOLA TURNIPS

An absolutely perfect heirloom turnip for simmering and then finishing with butter. Long and slender, violet and white.

HEIRLOOM RUTABAGAS

Usually in the baby form, but more elongate and more intense than turnips. Excellent raw or in soups, stews, purees, risotto, or roasted. Balance and complexity superior to that of turnips. We don't peel. Shelf (without tops) of 14-30 days.

CHINA ROSE RADISH

Classic pungent winter radish, best sliced but not peeled. Not at all mild. Very nice sliced thinly and smeared with brie, chevre, or butter. Can also be chopped and added to cold salads of cucumbers, greens, tuna, beans, or egg. Tops should be cooked like turnip greens.

FRENCH BREAKFAST RADISH

The most mild of radishes, fine any way you use a China Rose. Also really nice sliced thinly and in sandwiches of crusty bread, nice cheese, and/or roast beef, turkey, or ham.

WHITE ICICLE RADISH

Midway in pungency between China Rose and French Breakfast, with similar uses. Probably related to the daikons.

Winter Squash

Winter squash are not squash grown during the winter. They are squash grown in the warm months and harvested in August or later, but that have thick skins that let us store these for later use. Some can even keep until winter. We grow only a few kinds because we are beset with certain insect pests, so expect only Courge Longue de Nice (the manila-hued winter form), spaghetti squash, and butternut squash.

All winter squash are best stored in a pantry, basement, or on the counter, NOT refrigerated until they are cut.

These squashes are traditionally baked or simmered in stews, but modern chefs are exploring other cooking techniques that well show off the eating qualities of these harbingers of autumn. Butternut squash soup is now a standard item on many autumn restaurant menus.

Our absolute favorite winter squash, the elite Courge Longue de Nice, shares many culinary characteristics with sweet potatoes. Both have deliciously creamy, rich, sweet flesh that is very suited to baking or roasting. Both are versatile in the kitchen and can be treated as either a savory vegetable or starch or used as a base for sweet pies. Both have skins which, when the crops are properly grown and only briefly stored, are tender, tasty, packed with vitamins, and offer nice textural contrast to the soft flesh (this winter squash is the only variety we know of that has such tender skin that one can easily eat). Both courge and sweet potatoes are rich in vitamin A, but sweet potatoes then take off into a nutritional class of their own, being rich in vitamin C and beta carotenes and high enough in protein, calcium, iron, and other minerals to serve as a sole food source. For our farm, the harvests of Courge Longue winter squash and sweet potatoes are a celebration that marks, with sometimes gloriously generous yields, the beginning of the end of the hot, steamy summer months.

The winter squash form of **courge** often comes to you de-seeded. We cut the bulbous end off of each massive squash because this superior cultivar is not offered for sale in any US seed catalogs, and we often need every last seed for the next year's planting. De-seeding also saves the customer money, mess, and trouble, as scooping the stringy seed mass out of winter squash is necessary before cooking but is hardly to everyone's taste. You often get only pure usable flesh, protected by skin that nicely softens upon cooking.

Store in the refrigerator once cut, and gently wipe any field soil from the skin with a damp cloth before cooking.

Sweet Potatoes

Even' Star Organic Farm has the lovely soils and long growing season that helps our sweet potatoes be among the best grown anywhere. We harvest, wash, cure, and then carefully sort these, followed by storing them at 66° F such that the sweets slowly gain more and more flavor. Handled so well, our sweets easily keep from the October harvest until April or May. We sort and distribute sweet potatoes into two sizes. The "fingerlings" are more starchy, slender, narrow, shaped like a carrot, and outstanding left skin-on, chunked, and then roasted with garlic (recipe follows). Fingerling sweets do not keep as well as bigger ones, so use soon. The bigger sweet potatoes (from 4 oz. to as large as 3 to 5 pounds) are the most easily peeled for subsequent steaming, grating, or pie-making, but are also the fastest to chunk for a quick roast. Very large sweet potatoes are unjustly scorned by novices, but old-time Southern cooks treasure the mammoths for ease of use. They also know that a slowly grown but big sweet potato is more flavorful than a typical conventionally grown, smaller sweet potato whose growth was rushed and babied with agricultural chemicals. Sweet potatoes should be washed once more and then stored in the pantry or basement or countertop, NEVER in the refrigerator unless they've been cooked.

Different sweet potato cultivars have markedly different flesh colors and flavors. We usually grow:

- BEAUREGARD, orange, creamy, not too sweet, and with very full and nuanced flavors. Our absolute favorite orange type.

- COVINGTON, orange as well but so sweet that it oozes sugary syrup while cooking!

- WHITE HAMON, beige to milk-white and with a nutty, nuanced suite of flavors. Absolute best for frying but fine baked as well. Never boil

- JAPANESE PURPLE-SKIN White-Flesh is a great white sweet potato. Has typical nuttiness and subtlety, but has unique chestnut-like flavor if slowly baked past the softened stage.

- O'HENRY is smooth-skinned and mild; is most like Irish potatoes in texture and flavor.

Herbs And Flowering Greens

FLOWERING ASIAN MUSTARDS

Tender, fragrant, and sweeter than rapini. The more exciting heirloom parents to broccolini. Extremely popular with our restaurant accounts. They serve the sprigs raw, or in pasta's or simply sautéed with garlic. Hard to handle for retail due to very brief shelf life. Subscribers will receive these and/or arugula flowers only iced down, in coolers at the drop-off sites. March through May.

ARUGULA FLOWERS

Intense, versatile, and really popular with our restaurants, but of ephemeral shelf life. For adding to salads, sandwiches, risotto or pasta. We'll send subscribers these only in coolers, iced, at each coordinator's home. March and April.

CILANTRO

An herb many people adore and a similar number cannot abide. We use it in salads, salsas, marinades for grilled shrimp and rockfish, and of course in many Thai dishes, Chinese soups, and with vegetarian bean-and-rice burritos. Heating past 190°F kills most of the flavor. Ours is intense and cold-grown, with a shelf life much superior to store-bought cilantro.

CHERVIL

A classic French herb with a delicate flavor akin to a blend of nice parsley with sweet fennel. Outstanding in salads, or added late to sautéing chicken breast or white-fleshed fish. Makes an elite Dijon-based salad dressing. Heating past 210°F destroys most of the flavor.

HEIRLOOM DILL

Like all winter cold-grown herbs, with superior and balanced flavors relative to commercial herbs. Excellent in cold bean salads; in salads of greens, potato, cucumbers, or egg; mixed with sour cream for baked potatoes; in omelets; with dips for vegetables or in lemon-juice salad dressings; or with cooked fish or chicken dishes, added late. Heating past 210°F destroys most of the flavor, except when baked into breads.

Peachy Mama Peppers

Peachy Mama peppers are in a class by themselves. They originally hail from the Amazon basin. I renamed them to honor my mother and my wife, neither of whom can get enough of these treasures. Peachy Mamas are indescribably fragrant, especially when coarsely chopped (seeds and all) and gently sautéed in plenty of oil. Both the oil and pepper meats can then be used to flavor rice, eggs, cream cheese or soft goat cheese, pastas, or stews. The meats alone are outstanding on crusty bread as a unique appetizer. I advise subscribers to sauté as many of these as possible, cover generously with olive or vegetable oils, and put them up in mason jars in the fridge. Winter's dreariness can be much relieved with occasional treats such as Peachy Mamas.

Even' Star Poultry

We raise livestock on Even' Star Organic Farm because we believe that the old-fashioned integrated farm was a really good idea. Farm animals—in fact, nearly all the meats, milk, and eggs in the American diet—used to be free-ranging, humanely cared for, and fed primarily with pasture, hay, and crops too blemished to sell. There were no factory livestock operations with their inherently amoral treatment of animals, their antibiotics, their reeking waste lagoons, their disease problems, their implicit lack of respect either for the animals or for the human customers. We argue that the industrial livestock system is hideous, and wrong, and that farmers and consumers would do well to team up and demand an end to such an abomination. We commend the institutions such as the Humane Society that recognize that many people will remain omnivores but that also actively push for profound change in how America raises its meats.

We also hate to spray our vegetables, even with the organically-approved insecticides that are essential to the large Californian and Mexican organic operations. So we end up with between 30% and 40% of each harvest that is too ugly, from insect damage or bad weather, to sell. You don't see these tomatoes, watermelons, strawberries, or greens. But our livestock do, and happily convert these into foods that we and our loyal customers can treasure.

These are the reasons we raise laying chickens, stewing chickens and fryers.

HOW WE RAISE OUR CHICKENS: All of our birds range freely on large pastures, fenced to keep the birds out of the vegetables and predators out of the birds. Throughout their lives our animals are treated with compassion, dignity, and humanity. Our chickens eat grasses, clovers, bugs, and bushels of greens, sweet potatoes, tomatoes, melons, and other veggies that are too blemished to sell. As we cannot get organic corn in our area, we give the birds a very high-quality vegetarian grain mix (never with hormones, medications, or animal byproducts) specially formulated by us in partnership with our local Mennonite feed mill. Our birds are therefore not classed as organic—just very free range, very happy, very active, and very healthy.

When we successfully raise free-range fryers or roasters, these are much younger and more tender chickens than the stewing hens we used to offer when we had a very large flock of laying chickens. We will strive to offer at least one tender chicken per winter CSA subscription. In a yes-chicken delivery week, those CSA members who checked off "vegetarian" in their registration forms will receive extra vegetables valued at the same dollar amount as the chickens.

The differences between factory raised and ethically free ranged chicken are best expressed by Chef Julia:

> *A few years ago, I was driving through the Eastern Shore of Maryland and drove past a Perdue truck. If you have ever seen this, you might question eating commercially processed chicken in the future. The flat-bed truck transported the chickens, each in an individual cage, 20 cages high. The top chicken is, literally, living high on the hog. The poor chickens on the bottom were coated in droppings from the 19 layers on top. And the birds in the middle are breathing in a toxic fume. It's no wonder we have*

to worry about salmonella and other diseases in commercial chicken.

Farmer Brett also raises chickens. By contrast, these chickens are truly free-range. In fact, these chickens have more roaming room than most urban dwellers. And they eat better than most of us too – feasting on a rich diet of organic produce (the non-salable produce), weeds, grain and left-over food from the house. The chickens never receive antibiotics because they are not exposed to disease. Nor do they need growth hormones – they grow the old-fashioned way – with a healthy diet and plenty of exercise.

The chickens serve an important function for the farm. In addition to the obvious eggs and eventual meat, the chickens also help prepare the soil by weeding and creating "natural" compost. The chicken coops are strategically positioned around the barn with adjustable fencing that allows Brett to move the chickens. The chickens happily peck away at the weeds leaving a barren plot. To supplement their diet of weeds and grains, they act as a repository for non-salable produce and left-over food scraps from the house (all the things the rest of us would compost). In exchange, they enrich the soil with nitrogen generated from their, ahem, droppings. Further soil amendments are not required.

Let's be honest, though, Brett raises chickens for the eggs and the meat. The soil enhancement is a bonus. Once the hens reach menopause, and stop laying eggs, they are "converted" into stewing chickens.

As one might expect, the meat has more flavor -- the result of all that exercise. The "meat", the primary portion we eat from animals, is muscle – and they've developed just like ours when we go to the gym. The meat is darker (from all the blood flow) and with more texture (a euphemism for tougher). The eggs have a firmer texture too. They cook more quickly and fluffy than eggs purchased at the supermarket. The yolks are deep yellow, almost orange.

Over the years, I have taught many aspiring chefs and home cooks how to butcher a chicken. It's pretty straightforward, I tell them, as long as you cut in the right place: the ligaments are soft and the bones thin. My first attempt at cutting up a chicken from the farm was surprisingly difficult. After a few struggled attempts of redefining butchery, I realized that all the exercise that makes the meat more flavorful, also makes the ligaments and bones stronger.

A fryer chicken, even in the free-range environment, still has some tenderness, because they're only 6 weeks old. As such, they don't require as much special attention when cooking. These menopausal hens, at 3 years, need a slow cooking to tenderize and soften the meat.

IN YOUR FARMER'S WORDS:

Meats from free-ranging animals can be a radical departure from factory-raised supermarket meats. Older free-ranging birds can be very tough if cooked as you would a confined factory bird. Even younger fowl, such as our turkeys and roasting chickens, can have a tad more chew than supermarket fare. But the flavors are incredibly superior. And tenderness can easily be had by appropriate cooking. We cover that in the detailed recipes and strongly advise you to use these techniques.

CHAPTER 2:
Storing Your Produce for Optimal Freshness

We have prepared this list to help both summer and winter CSA members best enjoy our foods, and time which foods to eat first when you pick up your boxes each week. The chart covers all the seasonal foods we grow over the course of a year, and is not meant to imply that any one season could include all of the foods listed.

We have used our decades of experience as restaurant chefs to advise you on how to best store your foods. While there are numerous beliefs on correct storage, the approaches that follow have been tested on many thousands of cases of wholesale produce.

Most fruits and vegetables can be grouped into simplifying categories that really help busy home cooks:

Produce that wants to be kept as cold as possible without freezing and preferably in a lidded container like a large Tupperware. Examples are most leafy greens, ripe berries, cucumbers, and radishes.

Produce that hates any refrigeration and wants a cool (or room temperature) pantry, basement, or kitchen. Examples are sweet potatoes and winter squash.

Produce that wants the warmer part of the fridge but that suffers if too cold. Includes basil, sorrel, and a few others.

Produce that likes refrigeration but that can briefly be kept on the counter. Examples are watermelon and carrots.

Fruits that need ripening, but that once ripe must be eaten soon or refrigerated. This group is the most complex and takes the most care. Refrigeration in these fruits will irreparably destroy the ripening enzymes within the fruits, thus dooming the foods to be under ripe and boring shadows of what they could have become. Examples include peaches and nectarines, but premature cooling of commercial tomatoes has made more Americans dissatisfied with mass-marketed tomatoes than with any other crop. Whenever possible, fruits in this category should be placed on a counter, slightly separated from each other, and not on their bellies but rather on their shoulders. The shoulders, most obvious with big tomatoes, are the part that surrounds where the stem was (or is). Once ripened at room temperature, fruits in this group are at the peak of flavor. At this point they must be eaten very soon or refrigerated, as rotting will begin within 12 to 24 hours. A refrigerated ripe tomato or nectarine or avocado will keep for a few days and is much better than one that festers on the counter until thrown out. To maximize flavors, refrigerated ripe fruits are often brought back to room temperature before eating.

Storage areas also have subtle temperature differences that can also help you keep foods best:

The **coldest areas of the fridge** are usually the bottom, back, and crisper drawers; the door shelves are generally the warmest (e.g. better for basil)

Basements are usually cooler than pantries or closets. If dry, they are excellent for winter squashes and sweet potatoes.

Windowsills ripen tomatoes much faster than countertops.

Enjoy your great local fruits and vegetables, and store them well!

Basil, all types -- Shelf Life: 2-5 days
Cut stems in vase with water on countertop is best, or in the warmest part of the refrigerator. Excessives cold blackens the leaves.

Blackberries -- Shelf Life: 3-5 days
Must be refrigerated: coldest part of fridge. If storing in a plastic container, pack loosely. It's also okay to store in an open container. Wash right before eating/using. Excess water leads to fungal growth.

Brussels Sprouts -- Shelf Life: Keeps 3-4 weeks
Coldest part of the fridge.

Cabbage -- Shelf Life: Refrigerated up to 4 months
Best anywhere in the fridge. Can be stored in a very cold basement if needed, but not ideal.

Cabbage - Chinese -- Shelf Life: 5-21 days
Any part of fridge.

Carrots -- Shelf Life: 3 months, properly stored
Coldest part of the fridge. Best to store dry (in a bag). If they are too wet they will start to sprout or rot. Out of the bag they begin to go flaccid. Cellar only with great care.

Chives -- Shelf Life: 4 - 7 days
Dry, loose in a plastic bag in the coldest part of the refrigerator. Wash just before using.

Cilantro -- Shelf Life: 3 - 14 days
Washed, drained and then refrigerated. In a sealed Tupperware, with a paper towel or cloth underneath to help regulate the moisture.

Cucumbers -- Shelf Life: 3-10 days
Refrigerate.

Dill -- Shelf Life: 3 - 14 days
Washed, drained and then refrigerated. In a sealed Tupperware, with a paper towel or cloth underneath to help regulate the moisture.

Eggplant -- Shelf Life: 7-10 days upon refrigeration
On counter until ripe and soft (and a little wrinkly) -- this is sweetest and most tender. When ripe put in fridge.

Fennel Bulbs -- Shelf Life: 1 - 3 weeks
Coldest part of fridge. Leaves like to be dry in a bag. Stems like to be loose in a bag.

Greens:
All greens should be washed and drained before storing in the refrigerator. Longest shelf life is had by placing greens on top of a paper towel or clean cloth inside of a lidded Tupperware container. Whole heads store longer and better than cut leaves.

Arugula – Shelf Life: 3 - 14 days
Collards – Shelf Life: 3 - 14 days
Cress – Shelf Life: 3 - 7 days
Kale – Shelf Life: 3 - 14 days
Lettuce – Shelf Life: 3 - 7 days
Mesclun – Shelf Life: 2 - 5 days
Mustard Greens – Shelf Life: 3 - 10 days
Pac Choi – Shelf Life: 3-21 days
Sorrel – Shelf Life: 1 -7 days
Tat Soi – Shelf Life: 1 - 3 weeks

Leeks -- Shelf Life: 5 - 30 days
Coldest part of fridge, loose and dry in plastic bag.

Mint -- Shelf Life: 2-5 days
Cut stems in vase with water on countertop is best, or in the warmest part of the refrigerator. Excessives cold blackens the leaves.

Okra -- Shelf Life: 3-7 days
Refrigerated, dry and loose in bag.

Onions (green and spring) -- Shelf Life: 3-14 days
Must be refrigerated.

Oregano -- Shelf Life: 2 - 5 days
Do not wash! Store loose in a bag in the warmest part of refrigerator. Best if used immediately.

Parsley -- Shelf Life: 4 - 21 days
Washed, drained and then refrigerated. In a sealed Tupperware, with a paper towel or cloth underneath to help regulate the moisture.

Peppers (Green - Sweet) -- Shelf Life: 1 - 5 weeks
Refrigerate, loose and dry.

Peppers (Red - Sweet) -- Shelf Life: 3 - 21 days
Refrigerate, loose and dry.

Potatoes (Irish) -- Shelf Life: Up to 4 months in fridge, 6 weeks in pantry
Pantry, cellar or warmest part of the fridge. Very cold temperatures lead to increased sugar/sweetness; nice for some people, unexpected for others. New potatoes, on the other hand, must be refrigerated.

Potatoes (sweet) -- Shelf Life: 5 weeks - 8 months, depending on variety and previous handling
Hate refrigeration: NEVER in fridge. Basement or Pantry. Ideally at 55 - 65F, but tolerates up to 80F or higher.

Radishes -- Shelf Life: 1 - 5 weeks
Washed, drained and then refrigerated, in a Tupperware, with a paper towel or cloth underneath to help regulate the moisture.

Rutabaga -- Shelf Life: 2 - 7 weeks
Loose and dry in any part of the refrigerator.

Squash Blossoms -- Shelf Life: 1-3 days
Refrigerate ASAP! Store in a lidded tupperware with a moist papertowel in the bottom.

Squash, Summer (ALL) -- Shelf Life: 3-10 days
Refrigerate.

Squash, Winter (Butternut, Spaghetti) -- Shelf Life: 3 weeks - 4 months
In a cool basement (55 -65F). Hate refrigeration.

Tarragon -- Shelf Life: 4 - 7 days
Dry, loose in a plastic bag in the coldest part of the refrigerator. Wash just before using. You can also pack it in vinegar upon receipt -- it will keep indefinitely that way.

Tomatoes, Big Slicing -- Shelf Life: Once ripened and refrigerated: 3 - 5 days
Countertop, loose and separated on platter, until just soft. On shoulders as per peaches and nectarines.

Tomatoes, Cherry -- Shelf Life: In refrigerator: 7 - 10 days
Assuming they arrive ripe, eat within 12 hours or refrigerate. If underripe, store in open container on counter until fully ripe.

Tomatoes, Plums -- Shelf Life: In refrigerator: up to 10 days
Store loose on counter, separated from each other, until ripe. Use or refrigerate within 24 hours.

Turnips -- Shelf Life: 2 - 7 weeks
Loose and dry in any part of the refrigerator.

Watermelon -- Shelf Life: 3 - 5 weeks
Counter storage will not help ripening, but much more tolerant of pantry, fridge or basement storage than other melons.

CHAPTER 3: Key Techniques and Definitions of Terms

Baking And Roasting are infrequently used for the winter line-up of vegetables, with the wonderful exceptions of roasted turnips and rutabagas, baked sweet potatoes, and blanched greens that are then integrated within baked lasagna's or quiches.

Roasting is a subset of baking. In this simplest of cookbooks, roasting usually means adding seasoning and olive oil, baking between 340°F and 425°F until nearly soft, then adding (if desired) chopped onion, garlic, and herbs.

To Blanch is to briefly (10-90 seconds) steam or boil, usually followed by shocking. More used with the winter cooking greens.

Boiling is unjustifiably looked down upon as a "common" cooking technique. Boiling can make tough greens or old stewing chickens more tender than can anything except a pressure cooker. Boiling can also dispel or dilute the occasionally bitter flavors of some vegetables. I always add about 1 teaspoon salt per quart of water to preserve both the color and some of the nutrients that can be lost by none-careful boiling. Be sure, too, that the water is fully boiling (medium and small bubbles coming up from the pot's bottom) or rolling more vigorously. Simmering is a more gentle boil, with only small bubbles coming up. Simmering is the main technique for many a great tomato sauce.

To Braise is to cook under low to moderate heat, with plenty of water, broth, beer, or wine, until soft. May be done on stovetop or in oven, but add a lid or more fluid for the oven. Excellent for non-bitter, cold-season greens, for some meats, and for "comfort food" approaches. Cooking times vary from only 20 or 30 seconds (the most tender greens) to at least 20 minutes (turnips and rutabagas).

Grilling means cooking over an open flame and usually on top of a grate. We grill many summer vegetables: summer squash, plum tomatoes, skewered cherry tomatoes, tomatillos, Turkish Sweet Slicer peppers, sweet potato slices, and even par-boiled potatoes. Winter foods that are good grilled include Chinese Thick-Stem mustard, whole crowns of Maruba Santoh and tat soi, and sweet potato slices. Even at its simplest, good grilling of vegetables should involve brushing them sparingly with vegetable oil and seasoning with salt and pepper. More complex marinades can include soy sauce, wine, minced onion and garlic, herbs, ginger, etc.

Oil here means oil from vegetables, seeds, or nuts. I advocate using oils to protect broiling, grilling, or roasting foods from drying out, to better conduct heat in the context of grilling, and in the more traditional sense to prevent foods in a skillet from sticking. In the Italianate, light cooking that is my bias, I never fry or sauté in pure butter (a fat, not an oil), but rather sparingly use butter added late to a sauté process or even as a final seasoning.

I always stock 3 oils: extra-virgin olive oil, any relatively flavorless peanut, corn, or canola oil, and a dark sesame oil such as Kadoya. Extra-virgin olive oil is strongly perfumed, outstanding in salads or roasted vegetables, but easily burned and costly for sauté. Sesame oil acts in much the same way but is of Asian origin. I therefore blend either of the two strongly-flavored oils above with the intentionally neutral corn, peanut, or canola oil. The neutral oils elevate the temperatures at which the olive or sesame oils alone would burn, as well as decreasing cost and toning down the at times overwhelming flavors of the premium oils.

Poaching is a most temperature-sensitive, gentle technique. It means barely cooking greens, eggs, or most famously fish in water or broth that is just below 212°f and that is rigorously guarded against that boiling point. Poaching respects tender foods better than any other cooking approach, though with chewier or tougher foods boiling remains a better choice.

To Shock is an essential step that follows boiling or steaming of many foods, from tomatoes, greens, and other vegetables to eggs and even shrimp. Shocking stops the cooking process just where you want it by immediately plunging the really hot food into an ice water bath (recall that foods continue to cook from the time they are taken from the stove until the time they cool to room temperature). They are then drained promptly. This keeps the lovely bright green of asparagus, beans, and leafy vegetables, as well as keeping textures crisp rather than mushy. Nearly all vegetables and plain shrimp served in many restaurants are blanched and shocked, later seasoned, and possibly re-heated. Shocking gives busy cooks insurance against overcooking. Ice water is our friend.

Steaming is one of the hottest and fastest ways to cook, but adds little flavor (in contrast with sautéing or grilling). Western steamers are good, but a wok and stackable bamboo steamers, available in good Asian markets, remain my favorite. Be sure to start with at least ¾ inch of water for fast steaming and at least 3 cups of water for long steaming. Put your food in the steamer after it has fully heated up and is vigorously steaming.

Cooking Greens

The most common way we cook greens is to sauté them following blanching/shocking. The shocking may be omitted if the initial blanching is immediately followed by the sauté. Pre-wilting by blanching or steaming reduces the wateriness of the final dish and lets the other ingredients stay crisp. There are two basic approaches, Italian and Chinese, and each may be modified in countless ways. All involve coarsely chopping the greens and salting and peppering to taste, so these are implied but not spelled out in the following.

On Pots and Pans

I urge CSA members to consider pruning their kitchens of potentially hazardous cookware. As a chef, I used every conceivable type of pot, pan, and baking tray. But cookware coated with Teflon or other synthetics always slowly and imperceptibly losing their finish, and molecules of Teflon are now routinely discovered in alarming amounts in human tissues and in the environment. Enameled pots (e.g. Le Creuset) are outstanding, but only if the enamel finish is entirely intact. I am pretty certain that I have some of the heavy metals in my bones that were originally coatings, cast onto pots that in my thriftiness I continued to use even when the enamel layer began to chip. Less strident cautions are apt for solid aluminum pots. Aluminum appears to be OK except for acidic cooking (like tomato sauce) but data on the health effects of aluminum are ambiguous.

So what pans to use? Cast iron makes the absolute best for skillets and woks, and cultures that still favor cast iron have lower incidences of anemia (any iron that leaches out into your food acts as a vital nutrient; not so with aluminum or Teflon). The only drawbacks are that iron pans weigh more and react with acidic foods. For deep frying and large volumes of stew I use cast iron Dutch ovens, though I carry these with two hands when full.

And for boiling water, as well as all sizes of saucepans, high-quality (i.e., thick) stainless steel is super.

Finally, having both a blender and a food processor will make cooking much easier. I loathe any surplus of kitchen gadgets but find these indispensable. It should also be noted that a blender makes a poor substitute for a food processor, and a food processor rarely purees as smoothly as a blender – hence the need for both.

ABBREVIATIONS

Most of these are standard in U.S. cookbooks.

t = teaspoon

T = tablespoon

c = cup

temp = temperature, °F

s and p = Kosher or sea salt, plus ground black pepper, to taste. Good starting points are 1 t salt and ½ t black pepper per 4 people being served, but use your own judgment and taste. Farmers out in the sun all day may be poor judges of salt needs for people with other lifestyles.

CHAPTER 4: The Detailed Recipes

Basic Italian Sautéed Greens

1 bag (gallon) of pre-washed kales, collards, stir-fry blend, mustards, Italianate wilting blend, etc.

¾" water to steam or 2 quarts salted water to boil

Ice bath (see "Shocking" section in the Key Techniques chapter)

1 ½ t olive oil + 1 ½ t neutral oil

2 – 4 cloves garlic, coarsely chopped

s and p to taste

Barely wilt greens in steamer or by blanching; shock in ice bath if you'll not immediately sauté. Drain. Coarsely chop. Sauté by heating garlic in oils until garlic edges have just started to brown, and IMMEDIATELY dump drained greens into the skillet. Stir around and sauté about 30 more seconds. Will cool quickly, so a lidded serving dish is apt.

Variations Of The Basic Italian:

a) Delete the garlic, and substitute for it slivered onions, half-moons of yellow summer squash or zucchini, and/or sweet red pepper pieces.

b) Keep garlic and onions, and add 1 T butter or ½ c heavy cream to the skillet when the greens are almost done. Serve with toasted chopped almonds, or whole toasted pine nuts, on top.

c) Add fresh sage or rosemary to the hot skillet the second before adding the greens.

Basic Chinese Sautéed Greens

Use the exact same ingredients as the basic Italian, but exchange the olive oil with toasted sesame oil (e.g., Kadoya), substitute 1 T soy sauce for the last salt, and sauté 1 t fresh minced ginger with the garlic. Proceed as per the basic Italian.

<u>Variations Of The Basic Chinese:</u>

a) Add more vegetables, especially 1 ½ " pieces of scallion or Egyptian onion, sliced Brussels sprouts, sweet red pepper, etc.

b) Add pre-cooked, drained udon, Asian vermicelli, or ramen noodles to the skillet when the greens are nearly done. Increase seasoning appropriately.

c) Add 2-3 beaten eggs to the sautéing greens; cook to scramble. Serve over steamed rice and re-season. Excellent boost for people just recovering from sickness.

Button Mushrooms And Greens

This is excellent served on its own with crusty bread, or freshly boiled potatoes or baked potatoes. It is also lovely served over pasta or alongside chicken or scallops. Generous addition of freshly ground black pepper can really highlight all the flavors.

1 gallon prewashed greens: kale, collards, stir-fry blend, mustard greens or Swiss chard

½ onion sliced

1 pint button mushrooms (portobello or crimini would also work well), sliced ¼ inch thick

1 tsp salt, plus salt and pepper to taste

2 tsp olive oil

2 cloves garlic

¼ cup white wine

1 ½ cup heavy cream

1. Pre-blanch and shock the greens: in a large pot of boiling, salted water, cook greens until just wilted, approximately for 1 minute and drain. Shock in an ice bath, and drain well.
2. Coarsely chop greens if desired, or leave whole.
3. In a large skillet, add oil. Over medium high heat, cook onions and garlic until barely translucent. Add the mushrooms and continue cooking for 1 minute more, stirring often.
4. Add white wine to mushroom pan and simmer for 2 minutes.
5. Add cream and continue cooking to reduce for 5 more minutes, until approximately 1 cup of liquid remains.
6. Add the greens, stir well, adjust seasoning with salt and freshly ground black pepper. Cook only until greens are heated through, about 30 seconds.

GINGER SESAME FUSION GREENS

This recipe also works well with Swiss chard, though the greens should be cut into 1 inch pieces instead of being left whole.

(serves 4-6)

3 large or 6 small heads bok choi, pac choi or michihili

3 cloves garlic, peeled and chopped

1 teaspoon fresh ginger, minced

2 tablespoon dark roasted sesame oil (such as Kadoya brand)

2 tablespoons mild soy sauce, or 1 tablespoon double dark soy sauce

¼ teaspoon (or more depending on taste) black pepper

2 tablespoons butter

¼ cup sake or white wine

1. Cut whole heads in half and rinse thoroughly.
2. In a large skillet, heat sesame oil over medium heat. Add garlic and ginger, sauté for 2 minutes, or until garlic just begins to soften. Add greens, cut side down, and pepper.
3. Cover the greens and steam for 1 minute. Add sake or white wine and soy sauce.
4. When inner core is just soft (about 3 minutes, depending on size), add butter. Shake pan to incorporate.
5. Adjust seasoning with salt and lemon juice if necessary.

CLASSIC SOUTHERN-STYLE GREENS

This staple of the American South is still great comfort food. We advise seeking out the absolute best bacon or ham you can find; most commercial types such as Smithfield and Armour have lots of water and chemicals added.

1 bag (appr. gallon Ziploc) pre-washed collards, kales, mustards, stir-fry blend, etc., coarsely chopped

¼ - ½ lb bacon, ham, or sausage, raw but coarsely chopped

1 onion, sliced or chopped

½ t black pepper

salt only after tasting

1. Bake meat in heavy skillet at 350°F until crisping at edges. Pour off most of fat but retain at least 2 T. Add onion and continue baking until onions and meat are fully cooked.
2. Carefully remove from oven, add greens, and sauté until greens are just wilted or beyond. Season. May also add a touch of vinegar.
3. Nice served with sweet potato, herbed grits, or mashed potato. we was encouraged to join my hosts in bourbon and soda (not wine or beer) the first time we was served this dish properly fixed, and that beverage still fits.

KOSHER EQUIVALENT TO THE SOUTHERN-STYLE GREENS

A worthy take on the above deletes the pork, and substitutes ground beef (not too lean), coarsely chopped and parboiled brisket, or (my preference) boneless but skin-on, coarsely chopped pieces of chicken thigh. The breast won't do it justice: it is too dry a cut. All other procedures and ingredients are the same. The chicken lightens the dish considerably relative to the pork or beef.

Vegetarian Equivalent To The Southern-Style Greens

The basic Southern-style is even fit for a meatless approach. Sauté 2 sliced up onions in 2 T oil under moderate flame until fully caramelized (browning at edges, or more); consider adding 1 T tamari. Then proceed as per the above. Particularly nice with fresh thyme added late, or fresh basil added after the cooking is all done.

Warm Salad Spin-Off Of Southern-Style Greens

If you use only the most tender of our cooking greens (e.g., the robust salad mix aka Italian wilting mix, stir-fry greens up until about April, tat soi or Pac choi), and if you let that out-of-the-oven skillet cool a bit more, a warm wilted salad can happen. Simply barely wilt the greens (about 5 seconds usually does it) in the skillet and immediately transfer to a cool serving dish. Then splash about 1 teaspoon red wine or cider vinegar into the skillet, loosen all the caramelized bits, and drizzle all over the greens. Particularly nice on blustery winter nights.

Curried Greens

1 bag (gal. Ziploc) pre-washed cooking greens

2 t vegetable oil

1 onion, chopped

1 clove garlic, chopped

¼ t whole cumin seed

½ - 1 t curry powder

s and p to taste

¼ c plain yogurt (optional)

Sauté onions, cumin seed and curry powder together until former are translucent, then add greens to cook until just wilted or beyond. Add yogurt if desired and reduce heat. Nice served alongside brown or Basmati rice, or with pan-fried potatoes.

Curried Greens Stuffing For Chicken

1 bunch mustard greens or other pre-washed cooking greens, coarsely chopped

½ cup raisins

½ stick butter

3 cloves garlic, sliced

1 ½ tsp curry powder

salt and pepper to taste

1. Melt butter in sauté pan. Add garlic. Cook for 2 minutes over medium heat, and add the curry powder. Cook for 2 more minutes and add the raisins.

2. Add the mustard greens. And cook until they wilt

3. Cool before using stuffing. Stuff under skin of chicken breast before baking.

Savory Vegetarian Greens And Potatoes

6 average sized russet potatoes, washed but with skins on
salted water to cover
1 bag (gallon) any of our cooking greens
3 – 6 T mix of olive and neutral oils
3 cloves garlic, chopped
1 large onion, chopped
1 t black pepper
½ to 1 t salt
½ bunch scallions
fresh herbs, or 1 t dried oregano, basil, or rosemary

1. Gently boil potatoes until just cooked (skins aren't all coming off, and a sharp knife inserted into spud encounters a teeny resistance). Remove from pot with a slotted spoon. Let cool, then chop into bite-sized pieces. Use same water to barely blanch greens, and be sure to shock in an ice bath. Drain in colander, and push out all extra water. Chop coarsely. Set aside. In a heavy skillet (works best in seasoned cast iron), sauté onion and garlic 'til barely soft. Add potatoes and fry, scraping pan bottom often and adding more oil if needed. When potatoes have started to brown, add greens, herbs, and chopped scallion. Cook two minutes more. If needed, season further before serving: this should be hearty, not bland.
2. Can nicely be served with a dollop of sour cream, or of home-made guacamole, or with grated cheddar or Monterey jack, on top. Also really good with 1 teaspoon whole cumin seed (added to skillet right before spuds go in) in lieu of or in addition to other herbs. Hot peppers complement the latter approach well.

Greens Quiche

1 home-made or frozen pie crust, zero sugar if possible

1 gal. any of our pre-washed cooking greens

salted water to blanch

1 t olive oil

1 medium onion, chopped

2 T white wine

3 eggs (large, or that volume equivalent)

2 cups milk, half and half, or light cream

¼ - ½ lb. Gruyere, Cheddar, jack, mozzarella, or similar cheese, grated

2 T chopped fresh herbs such as chervil, parsley, dill, tarragon, or thyme, (or 1 t dry if fresh is not an option)

1 t salt

½ t black pepper

1. If making your own crust, consider adding ½ t dried thyme to the flour before cutting in the shortening. Pre-bake crust until barely brown at edges. Keep oven at 350°F. Meanwhile, blanch or steam the greens, shock, drain as thoroughly as possible, and chop medium or coarsely. Set aside. Sauté onion until translucent, add white wine, and simmer 1 more minute. Let cool. Make batter by beating together liquid dairy, eggs, s and p, herbs, and onion-wine mix.
2. Place drained chopped greens into pie shell. Sprinkle grated cheese over greens, then pour batter over all. Bake about 50 minutes, until center of quiche doesn't jiggle when you poke the pie pan's edge. Center of quiche should also be slightly raised and golden brown at this point. Remove from oven and let cool at least 10 and as many as 60 minutes before serving. Cooling gives clean edges to the crust and filling upon cutting and plating.

A particularly Italianate variant of this adds 3 cloves garlic to the sautéing onions, uses dry or fresh basil in lieu of other herbs, and sprinkles pine nuts atop the cheese before pouring in the batter.

Classic Italian Greens And Garlic Soup

Working outside on a winter farm has taught us the value of great simple soups on frigid days. This one works best with homemade chicken or turkey broth, but vegetarian or purchased stocks can also do nicely.

3 cloves garlic, chopped

1 t olive oil

¼ c white wine

1 quart good poultry or vegetarian broth

½ t black pepper

½ - 1 t salt

½ lb. tortellini, ravioli, capellini, egg noodles, etc.

1 gal. pre-washed cooking greens, coarsely chopped

1 t (per diner) pesto or chopped fresh basil (optional)

1 baguette or similar crusty bread (not really optional)

1 bottle good to very good wine, red or white

1. In large pot, sauté garlic in olive oil 'til soft; immediately add ¼ c white wine.

2. Add broth and bring to boil. Add pasta of your choosing, continue boiling 'til pasta is just cooked, remove pot from heat, and taste and adjust seasoning. (If meal will be delayed, remove pasta immediately with a slotted spoon. It easily overcooks.)

3. Stir in greens and immediately serve.

4. The good bread really complements the dish, as does the basil, stirred in by each diner. Commercial pesto is easier to get in the depths of winter than is fresh or frozen basil.

5. The wine is for you to drink, especially if you needn't return to work. A stellar variant of this appears in the section on stewing chickens.

Taillevent's Cream Of Cress Soup With Caviar

Patricia Wells describes Taillevent as "a place that my husband, Walter, and we reserve for special occasions." And she describes its watercress soup as "the perfect choice for a celebratory New Year's Eve dinner. Like so much of the fare at this august restaurant, this soup shines with simple elegance."

The restaurant location is unknown by your farmer, but we loathe plagiarism.

The recipe is a lot of work and is absolutely worth it. This is one of the finest soups I've ever eaten, and 90% of non-caviar lovers have added caviar to their second serving. It is adapted from National Public Radio.

THE LEEK AND STOCK BASE:

3 T unsalted butter

1 lb leeks, white and tender green portions, rinsed, halved, and thinly sliced

1 onion, peeled and finely chopped

Fine sea salt

1 qt homemade chicken stock

2 c heavy cream (or substitute whole milk)

THE CRESS:

3 T sea salt

1 gal. English cress or curly American mustard, or 4 bunches watercress, roots and stems removed; washed

THE CREAM:

1 c heavy cream

Juice of 1 lemon

Sea salt

Freshly ground white pepper (or black pepper, but this will leave flecks in an otherwise pure white cream)

2 T caviar Lumpfish works and is more ecologically defensible than sturgeon.

EQUIPMENT:

A 6-quart stockpot, a 6-quart pasta pot fitted with a colander, a food processor

1. In a 6-quart stockpot, combine the butter, leeks, onions, and a pinch of sea salt. Cook, covered and over low heat, until soft but not

browned, about 3 minutes. Add the chicken stock and cream. Simmer gently, uncovered, for 30 minutes.

2. Puree the soup in a blender, food processor, or with a handheld immersion blender until emulsified into a smooth-textured mixture.

3. Return the mixture to the saucepan, increase the heat to high, and bring to a gentle boil. Using a slotted spoon, skim off any impurities that may rise to the surface. Set this base aside. (This mixture can be prepared up to 1 day in advance. To store, cover and refrigerate.)

4. Prepare a large bowl full of ice water.

5. In a 6-quart pasta pot fitted with a colander, bring 4 quarts water to a boil over high heat. Add the sea salt and the greens. Blanch, uncovered, until soft and wilted, 2 to 3 minutes. Immediately remove the colander from the water, drain the cress, and plunge the colander into the ice water to stop the cooking. Drain again, and puree the cress in a food processor. Place the puree in a fine-mesh sieve, and carefully press out (and discard) any remaining liquid. Set the puree aside.

6. In the bowl of a heavy-duty mixer fitted with a whisk (or with a handheld mixer), whip the cream at high speed until stiff. Add the lemon juice, and season to taste with sea salt and white pepper. Set aside.

7. At serving time, reheat the soup base until simmering. Remove it from the heat and add the cress puree, stirring until thoroughly blended. Serve the soup in warm, shallow soup bowls, placing a scoop of the whipped cream in the center of each bowl. Top with a small spoonful of caviar, and serve.

6 servings

Rapini With Grapes And Honey

The sweetness of the grapes balances nicely with the bitterness of the rapini. This is a wonderful side dish for grilled lamb or quail.

1 bunch rapini, coarsely chopped

1 tomato, sliced thin

1/4 tsp. chili flakes

1 tsp. olive oil

1/2 tsp. cumin

1 cup grapes, sliced

2 tbs. honey

salt and pepper, taste

Heat a skillet with honey. When honey begins to simmer, add cumin. Toss with grapes. Heat another large sauté pan. Add oil. Add chili flakes, then tomato and rapini. Cook for 3 minutes, stirring occasionally, until rapini turns bright green. Season with salt and pepper. Toss with grapes.

Rapini (Or Napini) With Toasted Sesame Seeds And Ginger

1 quart Ziploc rapini or napini

2 tsp. raw sesame seeds

1 tsp. sesame oil

1 tsp. fresh ginger, chopped

1 clove garlic chopped

1 tbs. sake or mirin

1 tsp. butter (opt.)

1 tsp. soy sauce

1. In a dry skillet, over medium heat, toast sesame seeds until golden brown. Immediately add sesame oil and garlic. Sauté until garlic just starts to brown.
2. Add ginger, and cook for 10 seconds. Add the rapini. Then add the sake and soy sauce. Cook until just barely wilted. Remove from heat. Stir in butter.

If weather conditions make the rapini slightly bitter, a touch of honey or sugar add with the greens can make the dish more balanced.

Rapini With Sausage And Pasta

1 lb. sweet Italian or lamb sausage, sliced

1 tablespoon olive oil

1 bunch rapini

2 garlic cloves, chopped

½ teaspoon chili flakes

¾ pound pasta – penne or linguine or other favorite shape.

¼ cup freshly grated parmesan

Salt pepper and lemon juice to taste.

1. Wash rapini and coarsely chop.
2. Heat a large skillet over high heat. Add half the olive oil and sausage. Cook sausage until it starts to brown. Remove from skillet and set aside.
3. To the same pan, add the remaining olive oil garlic and cook over medium heat until it starts to brown. Add the rapini and cook for 2 to 4 minutes more, or just until it turns bright green. Stir occasionally.
4. Meanwhile, bring a large pot of water to a boil. Season with salt and cook pasta according to package directions.
5. When pasta is done, strain the water, reserving about ¼ cup.
6. Toss pasta with sausage, rapini and cheese. If it seems dry, add some pasta water (or extra virgin olive oil).
7. Season to taste with salt, pepper and lemon juice.

Recipes For The Root Vegetables

Growing up as a child we most disliked the root vegetables. Our family used store-bought rutabagas the size of softballs, radishes from the produce section that were mealy, and turnips that were tasty only if cooked for a long, long time.

I have since learned that slow growing of root vegetables coupled with choosing excellent varieties can produce really nice additions to snacks and meals. We grow 3 basic types: radishes, turnips, and rutabagas.

Grate or slice any of the winter root vegetables, raw, into salad for flavor and textural contrasts. For snacking, thinly sliced (but not peeled) radishes, turnips, and rutabagas are excellent dipped into soy sauce, hummus, or one of the following dips. Additionally, thin slices of radish were practically made for smearing with butter, brie, chevre, etc. as an appetizer, and can be more exciting to guests than the inevitable crackers.

Curry Dip For Raw Vegetables

¼ c plain yogurt or sour cream

1 t curry powder

1 T minced raw onion

¼ t sea or Kosher salt

1 T freshly squeezed lemon juice

cayenne and/or ground cumin, optional and to taste

Mix thoroughly. Keeps 14 days in 'fridge if covered.

Sesame-Soy Sauce Dip

¼ c mayonnaise

1 T sesame seeds, toasted and cooled

1 – 2 T tamari or soy sauce

Mix thoroughly. Keeps 14 days in 'fridge if covered.

Spicy Salsa Dip

¼ c plain yogurt or sour cream

2 tablespoons good salsa

Tabasco or hot sauce to taste

salt to taste

1 T chopped cilantro

Mix thoroughly. Keeps 8 days in 'fridge if covered.

Cooking Turnips And Rutabagas

Cooking turnips and rutabagas lets them show their mellow complexity. Both are traditionally diced and added to long-simmering soups and stews to bring great depth and background not available from other vegetables. From Japanese miso soups to Italian minestrone to Scotch broth (yes, even Campbell's adds these), turnips and rutabagas are often core participants.

A second way people use these two are to simmer them with potatoes or winter squash, then mash them with butter, cream, salt and pepper. Use any good recipe for mashed potatoes, but substitute 1/3 – ½ of the potatoes with unpeeled turnips or rutabagas.

I like the above, but often want to enjoy pure turnips and rutabagas. Three nice recipes follow that do this.

Tender Turnip/Rutabaga Vinaigrette

2-3 cups washed, trimmed, but unpeeled baby turnips and/or rutabagas

water to cover, in a lidded pot

1 t salt

any good vinaigrette salad dressing (see salad section of greens), or vinegar and oil

s and p

Simmer the roots until just tender in the salted water (about 15 – 25 minutes). Drain. Let cool. Add generous amounts of the salad dressing, or drizzle with vinegar and olive oil. Taste for salt and especially more black pepper. Excellent as an alternative to green salads, or as a small appetizer preceding a heavy meal.

Turnips/Rutabagas In Butter

A nice comfort food for cold nights.

Cook the roots as above, or maybe in a chicken broth, but keep about a third of the simmering liquid in the pot once the roots are tender. Keep on a low simmer and add 1 T butter, ¼ t black pepper, and (optional) chopped parsley. Really good when you're not feeling so great. Goes very well with a baked potato.

Roasted Turnips/Rutabagas

This one has a deep European history and has recently become a staple in many of the better restaurants here in the US. The dish particularly complements heavier meat dishes, from Thanksgiving turkey to chicken or calves' liver to roasted beef, lamb, or pork. The mellow complexity of the roasted roots also adds unmatched character to vegetarian pasta or rice dishes.

a roasting pan

3 – 4 cups washed, trimmed, but unpeeled baby turnips and/or rutabagas

3 T olive oil or a neutral oil – olive oil blend

1 t salt

½ t black pepper

2 t fresh chopped thyme or rosemary, or 1 t dry rosemary (whole leaf, not powder)

1 T chopped garlic

2 T chopped onion

Cut any larger roots into pieces about 1 ½" long; leave smaller ones whole. Place in roasting pan, add salt, pepper, and oils and toss around. Bake in a 350°F - 375°F oven, stirring occasionally, until only the very centers of the larger roots are still hard. Add garlic, onions, and herbs, and continue roasting until all roots are just soft. Many will have begun to caramelize (i.e., turn brown, shriveled, and sweet). The roots cool quickly, so serve soon or in a lidded bowl.

Pickled Turnips

This recipe comes courtesy of longtime subscriber Sherry Jones.

2 sliced garlic cloves
Thyme sprigs
1/2 tsp Greek oregano
1 bay leaf
2 tsp coriander seeds
2 tsp turmeric
1 tsp fennel seeds
1/2 tsp red pepper flakes
2 T salt
2 c water
1/2 c cider vinegar
1 T olive oil
1 lb small turnips, unpeeled, cut into wedges

Combine all in a bowl, stir to dissolve salt. Pack turnip wedges into a jar, pour in brine mixture. Screw on lid. Put jar on a shelf and turn it over every day for a week. After a week, refrigerate.

Turnip Bruschetta

This recipe comes courtesy of subscriber Jennifer LaRoche. She suggests serving it as an appetizer/hors d'oeuvre for a winter cocktail party or open house.

2 medium turnips

1 medium red onion

¼ (or less) olive oil

4 oz. prosciutto (opt.)

1 tbs. fresh rosemary (or 1 tsp. dried)

1 – 2 tbs. balsamic (more or less depending on how much olive oil used)

8 slices baguette

1. Dice the turnips and red onion.

2. In a medium skillet, heat olive oil over medium high heat. Add the turnips and onions and sauté for 10 minutes, or until onions or soft and turnips are tender.

3. Add the prosciutto (or a pinch ¼ tsp of salt) to the turnips, season with the balsamic vinegar and rosemary.

4. Toast the baguette.

5. Just before serving top each slice with turnip/prosciutto mix.

Winter Squash And Ginger Soup

1 winter squash, such as Courge Longe de Nice or butternut

1 celery stalk

1 carrot

1 onion

3 cloves garlic

1 inch piece of ginger

1 tbs. butter

8 cups water

½ cup cream (opt)

salt and pepper to taste

1. Cut squash in half. Roast in 350 oven with a little water for 1 hour, or until tender (a butter knife will pierce the flesh easily)

2. Meanwhile, cut onion, garlic, celery, carrot and ginger into small pieces.

3. Heat soup pot over medium heat and add butter. Add onions, let sit until they begin to turn golden, add garlic, ginger, carrots and celery. Stir for 2 minutes. Add water and salt.

4. When the squash is tender, scoop at the seeds, and discard. Scoop out pulp and add to soup. Puree.

5. Simmer for 10 more minutes to let flavors blend.

That Extra Loving Touch: Pickled Ginger And Apple Salad Over Crostini

1 tbs. pickled ginger + some of the juice

1 apple

1 bunch field cress

6 slices French bread, toasted

1. Core and slice apple. Toss ginger with apples and watercress. Top crostini with salad. Garnish soup with crostini.

Sauteed Spaghetti Squash With Capers And Garlic

This is excellent alongside seafood, beef, or vegetarian beans.

2 spaghetti squash

½ onion, peeled and sliced

3 garlic cloves, chopped

2 T olive oil

1 T capers

1 T butter

2 T white wine

Salt and pepper to taste

1. Cut spaghetti squash in half and scoop out the seeds and inner soft pulp with a large metal spoon. Place face down on a plate and microwave about 2 minutes per half (multiple batches should be necessary) until BARELY soft. If you lack a microwave, steam for about 6 minutes until just soft. Let cool, then plunge a fork longitudinally through the inside flesh and work it from end to end to make the "spaghetti". Use a metal spoon to get out the last strands.

2. Meanwhile, sauté onion with garlic in olive oil until just soft. Add capers, stir around, and then add spaghetti squash, 1 tablespoon butter, and ½ teaspoon each salt and pepper, or to taste. Sauté for about 3 minutes more at moderate heat, then finish with white wine.

Basic Baked Courge

This is fine as a simple, low-fat vegetable or starch, or as the preliminary cooking step prior to making a pie.

Each 4" or 5" courge "cylinder" serves two.

1. Halve the squash longitudinally and rub ¼ teaspoon vegetable oil or olive oil on the flat flesh side of each half, and sprinkle each with about ¼ teaspoon Kosher or sea salt. Place the cut flesh side down on a heavy cookie sheet or on a cast iron pan.

2. Bake uncovered at 350° until an inserted knife encounters little resistance (about 40 to 55 minutes, depending on squash thickness). Serve as is or with butter, herbs, or even with maple syrup and freshly ground black pepper. When using this approach as the first step for a pie, omit any later additions of more salt.

Basic Whole Baked Sweet Potatoes

Bake one 5" long sweet potato, or a similar chunk cut from bigger sizes, per person in a 375°F oven about 40 to 55 minutes, until a squeezed one is fully soft. Serve with the same accompaniments as the courge.

Sweet Potato Fries

These are really easy, just like French fries.

Assume 2 medium sweet potatoes will serve one person. Trim any bad spots from clean sweet potatoes but do not peel. Bake whole at 350° until just soft (cooking too long will lead to hollow sweets that break apart upon frying). Let cool. At this point, the baked sweets can be refrigerated as is for up to six days before using.

To fry: slice each sweet potato into French-fry size strips, leaving the skin on. Deep-fry until they float and have gotten a bit brown. Drain, sprinkle with salt (optional) and serve. Good condiments are hot sauce and ketchup

Chunked Roasted Sweet Potato With Garlic

Cut fingerling sweet potatoes or larger sweet potatoes into 1" chunks, left skin-on (3 cups of chunks serves 3 or 4, and this recipe follows that volume). Drizzle 2 t olive oil or veg. oil on top, and then stir in about ½ t salt and ¼ t black pepper. Microwave for 4 minutes, or skip this step and just roast in a heavy pan at 400°F until the edges start to soften. Add 1-2 t chopped garlic and (optionally) ½ c chopped onions and/or ½ t chopped fresh rosemary, sage, or oregano. Lower heat to 350°F and continue roasting until garlic has slightly browned and sweet potato has softened, about 8-10 minutes.

Sumptuous Sweet Potato Salad

This recipe comes courtesy of* The Good Earth Natural Food Co.*, in Leonardtown, MD. If you visit or live in the area, we encourage you to support our local grocer.

Dressing

½ c. extra virgin olive oil

2 T pure maple syrup

2 T orange juice

2 T sherry or balsamic vinegar

1 lime, juiced

2 t minced fresh ginger

½ t ground cinnamon

¼ t nutmeg

¼ t cardamom

Salad

6 lb Beauregard or other orange variety sweet potato, peeled and cut into ¾ inch cubes

¼ cup olive oil

1 c chopped scallions

1 c chopped fresh parsley

1 c pecans, toasted and coarsely chopped

1 cup raisins, brown or golden, or mix of both

Salt and pepper to taste

1. For the dressing, whisk the ingredients together in a small bowl. Season to taste with salt and pepper.

2. Toss sweet potatoes with olive oil, salt and pepper. Lay them on baking pans in a single layer and roast in a 425 oven until tender, approximately 10 minutes. Let potatoes cool to room temperature.

3. Place sweet potatoes in a large bowl. Add green onions, parsley, pecans and raisins. Pour dress over and toss gently to blend. Adjust seasoning with salt and pepper.

Sweet Potato Or Courge Pie

I lifted this from that classic American kitchen aid,* the Joy of Cooking *by Irma Rombauer and Marion Becker, and urge any of you that lack a copy to get one. Eighteen years of being in charge of restaurant kitchens has left me still extremely appreciative of this simple but always useful text.

Pre-bake a pie shell, homemade or store-bought, until barely tan or brown. Then mix:

1 ½ c cooked courge or sweet potato, de-skinned and mashed

1 ½ c heavy cream or canned evaporated milk

½ c brown sugar

¼ c white sugar

½ t salt

1 t cinnamon

½ t dried ginger

1/8 t cloves, ground

4 slightly beaten eggs

1. Cook all this over a double boiler, as per custard, until it thickens. Then cool slightly and add 1 t vanilla or 2 T bourbon or dark rum, and pour the mixture into the baked pie shell. Refrigerate about 3 hours until firm, then serve with whipped cream.
2. Rombauer and Becker advise the above, but we always feel pressed for time and hence do the following:
3. Whip all the above in a Kitchen Aid mixer, similar electrical beater, or by hand. Pour into the pie shell and bake in a 325°F to 340°F oven until it sets (where a slight shake by you causes minimal waves in the filling, about 50 minutes). Let cool and serve. An even lighter, more frothy pie can be had by separating the eggs into yolks and whites, whipping the yolks into all else, and whipping the whites separately to the soft peak stage. Then fold the whites carefully into the rest of the filling and bake as above.

Vegetarian/Vegan Burgers

2 tbs. olive or canola oil

½ cup minced onions

3 cloves garlic, peeled and chopped

¼ cup fresh oregano

1 teaspoon salt

¼ teaspoon cayenne

2 cups cooked black beans, slightly mashed.

2 cups cooked sweet potatoes, mashed (preferably a mix of White Hamon and Beauregard)

Salt and pepper to taste

1. In a large skillet over medium-high heat, add 1 tbs. of the oil. Sautee the onions and garlic until just cooked. Immediately remove from heat.
2. Add to the onions, add the beans, oregano.
3. Sprinkle cayenne and salt on top of the mashed sweet potatoes. This helps to better disperse the seasoning.
4. Mix all ingredients together and chill for at least 45 minutes. Season to taste with salt and pepper
5. Once chilled, form patties approximately 1 1/2 inch thick, and 4 inches in diameter.
6. Heat a large skillet over high heat, add remaining oil. Fry patties until golden brown and crispy on both sides.

Serve with sour cream mixed with fresh cilantro, any cheese, or any condiment that you would normally serve with a beef burger. Best to serve with a toasted crusty bread such as baguette or Kaiser roll.

French Lemon-Garlic Vinaigrette

1/4 c freshly squeezed lemon juice (bottled juice won't work, so don't consider it)

1/2 c rice wine, cider, sherry, or red wine vinegar

1/2 c extra virgin olive oil, preferably Greek or Lebanese

¼ c peanut or corn oil

1 packet mixed fresh herbs, especially chervil and parsley or dill and parsley

2 large or five small cloves garlic

1 t salt

1/2 t ground black pepper

1 or 2 T Dijon-type mustard (optional)

Place all these in a blender and process for 15-30 seconds. Refrigerate if not used within 24 hours. Great with mesclun or cucumbers. Can also substitute cilantro for the fresh herb mix, in which case thin slices of onion added to the salad itself complements the cilantro well.

Berry Vinaigrette

Extra strawberry, blackberry, or raspberry jam can be used to make a superb salad dressing.

1 c high-quality berry jam

2 T oil

1 large onion, coarsely chopped

1 garlic clove

1 c sherry, rice, red wine, or balsamic vinegar

2/3 c olive oil or oil blend

1 T fresh thyme or 2 T fresh chervil

about 1 t each s and p

Carefully roast (in a heavy pan) the jam until half-evaporated, and at the same time roast (in a separate pan and with the 2 T oil) one coarsely chopped large onion and a garlic clove. Blend all of that stuff until smooth with the vinegar of your choice, the 2/3 c oil, and the herb(s) and seasoning. This dressing is suitable for all types of our salad greens and puts to shame the commercial raspberry dressings that are cloyingly sweet and weirdly thickened. A salad made with this dressing goes really well with a deep red wine like a syrah, petite syrah, Shiraz, zinfandel, or cabernet franc or cabernet sauvignon. Quite appropriate when the winter winds howl.

Simple Italian Salad Dressing For Mesclun

1 bag (approx. ¾ - 1 ½ cups) Provençal herb mix or Genoa basil

1 c balsamic or red wine vinegar

3/4 c peanut or corn oil

3/4 c extra virgin olive oil

2 t salt or 1/3 c soy sauce or tamari

½ t ground black pepper

5 cloves garlic

1/4 cup chopped sweet onion or 1 large bunch scallions or Egyptian onions

Remove the tougher stems from the herbs, peel the garlic, and coarsely chop the onions or scallions. Put these and all other ingredients in a blender and blend until smooth (less than 45 seconds). Pour into an old wine bottle, cork, and refrigerate. Keeps practically forever. Shake well before using.

GREAT CAESAR SALAD DRESSING

There are a lot of pretty bad Caesar dressings out there: too bland, too fishy, too oily, too heavy, too stale seem to be the distinct ways they generally fail. This recipe evolved to keep restaurant patrons really loyal to Caesar salads. As a chef I served this one to countless customers in four establishments. This recipe works so well because the assertive flavors are in a balanced dance; no one is dominant. If you make it, I urge you to not delete any component. They all depend on each other.

Total execution time is 20-30 minutes. This dressing keeps about 6 months refrigerated, and is best after the first day. The recipe makes about 3 cups of dressing, enough for many salads. You need:

a Cuisinart or similar food processor (not a blender)

1 really fresh egg, medium or large, and at room temperature

2 T peanut or corn oil

1 more cup peanut or corn oil

1 cup olive oil

½ bulb (i.e., many cloves) garlic, chopped

½ cup white wine: any varietal will do except sweet ones

1 can (2 oz.) flat anchovy filets packed in oil, or ½ tube anchovy paste (vegetarians could substitute ¼ -1/3 cup capers for this)

¾ t black pepper, ground

1 t Kosher or sea salt

2 t Worcestershire or soy sauce

juice of 1 ½ large, or 3 small, lemons

¾ cup freshly grated Romano, Parmesan, or aged Asiago cheese

¼ t Tabasco

2 t dried basil or ¼ cup chopped fresh basil or parsley

1. Sauté the garlic in the 2 T oil in a heavy skillet. When garlic edges just begin to brown, add the white wine. Simmer about 4 minutes more, until wine has reduced volume by about half. Let cool.
2. Meanwhile make a simple mayonnaise: crack the room-temperature egg into the Cuisinart and run at high speed with

the steel blade for 45 seconds, or until egg color is a pale yellow. Keep machine running, and very slowly pour in the two cups of oils in a thin stream (1/8" – ¼" wide). It should take about 45 seconds for the oils to be all added to the egg. You've now made unseasoned super-fresh mayonnaise.

3. Add the anchovies (plus their packing juices); pulse 15 seconds. Add all other ingredients except the cooked garlic and the lemon juice; pulse until all are incorporated (about 30 seconds). Then keep the machine running while slowly streaming in the lemon juice and garlic fluids, followed by a fast addition of the chopped garlic. Done.
4. Store in glass jar or plastic (never in metal).
5. Dress our salad greens, especially the Robust Salad Mix or pure tat soi, with this. A salad for four people would be about ½ lb of greens, 1 ½ - 2 tablespoons dressing, about ½ c seasoned croutons, and (optional) additional grated cheese, lemon wedges, 90-second hard-boiled eggs, or anchovy filets.

Dreamy Green Goddess

¼ cup tarragon leaves, fresh

4 tablespoons Egyptian onions, garlic chives, and/or baby leeks, washed and chopped

½ cup arugula leaves

½ c mayonnaise

2 tbs. sour cream

1 t capers

½ t white wine vinegar

s and p to taste

1. Combine herbs in a food processor, and process until coarsely chopped.
2. Add mayonnaise, sour cream and capers. Pulse machine until the mixture in just smooth.
3. Season with vinegar, salt and pepper.

Serving Suggestions: Excellent as a sauce for rockfish, grilled chicken, or grilled or blanched vegetables. It is also fabulous as a dipping sauce for Fried Okra, Zucchini or Eggplant.

Goma Dressing

8 tbs. sesame seeds, toasted and ground

2 tbs. sake

2 tsp sugar

2 tbs. soya sauce

1 tbs. rice vinegar

Mix everything together. Add a touch of hoisin if extra sweetness is desired.

Other Salads

Here are a few salads with great flavor and long traditions but that are served too rarely in the US. We put in **Bold** the defining essences of each salad.

Really fine cold-grown **Cilantro** can take center stage in a wonderful greens or tomato salad. One of my favorite versions for the winter is **cilantro** ripped coarsely into a salad of **Mesclun** (4-6 cups) and **Thinly Sliced Onion**, then dressed with 1 ½ t each **olive oil** and **lemon juice** or rice vinegar. Sprinkle with Kosher or sea salt and fresh black pepper. This turns the salad course into a major highlight.

Pungent complements sweet in the next group of winter salads. **Arugula** or **robust salad mix** can be interchanged in the following 3 classic Italian salads. Each can be dressed with either the French or the Italian dressings above. Alternately, lightly drizzle about 1 ½-2 t red wine or balsamic vinegar and 2 t olive oil, plus Kosher/sea salt and black pepper, right before serving.

a) Thickly line a pretty platter with bite-size pieces of the greens. Place freshly **roasted sweet red peppers**, or jar-type roasted sweet red peppers (packed in oil) on top. Sprinkle **Romano, Asiago, Parmesan, or feta cheese** on top. Dress. Best served with both knife and fork. Excellent for bitterly cold nights.

b) Rip up about 4 cups **arugula**, robust salad mix, or even our mesclun into a large salad bowl. Add thinly sliced and unpeeled local **apples**, especially Winesap, Stayman, Nittany, York, or Cameo varieties. Dress.

c) Substitute ripe **pear** slices for the apples, but add as well **chevre** or **Gouda**, and perhaps freshly toasted almonds, walnuts, or pecans. Dress.

Piquant is the essence of the next group. Use any of our **salad greens** and add **thinly sliced raw onion** and either **capers** or chopped stuffed **green olives.** Dress with the French or Italian dressings above, or squeeze fresh lemon and drizzle olive oil. Salt and pepper to taste. Especially good served in the European tradition, at the end of the meal, following heavier entrées that need lightening. Pinot Grigio wines or amber beers also do well alongside.

Finally, from Japan comes a lightly cooked, then chilled, sesame-driven salad that is great with any of our greens except pure arugula or mesclun when it has lettuce (e.g., deep-winter mesclun). Blanch and then shock a full gallon of any of the **stir-fry blends, kales, collards, mustards, robust, et al**. Toast 2 T **sesame seeds** in a heavy skillet until golden and they begin to pop. Add 2 cloves **garlic**, chopped, ¼ c sliced onion, and 1 T Kadoya sesame oil. Sauté gently until garlic is barely cooked; turn off heat. Add 2 T **soy sauce**, 1 t freshly chopped **ginger**, ½ t black pepper, 2 t rice vinegar, and 2 t sugar or 1 t honey. Toss with now-cold greens and let sit to adsorb flavors. Add salt and freshly squeezed lemon juice to taste right before serving.

Cilantro-Lemon Marinade

For grilling rockfish, grouper, shrimp, chicken or turkey breast or, for vegetarians, zucchini, Chinese thick-stem mustard, tat soi or other heads of Asian mustards, pre-boiled potatoes or firm tofu. Marinates enough to serve four.

½ bunch cilantro
2 T fresh lime or lemon juice
1 ½ t chopped garlic
3 T chopped Egyptian onion or scallion
1 t salt
1 t black pepper
2 T olive oil
2 T white wine or beer
1 T soy sauce

Mix. Marinate seafoods or poultry for at least 2 hours, and vegetables for 45-60 minutes. While the food is grilling, occasionally spoon some of the marinade onto it. Serve with freshly made salsa (mango, tomato, etc.) whenever possible.

Classical Robust Wine-Herb Marinade

For grilling meats, poultry, mushrooms, eggplant and many other vegetables. Marinates enough to serve four.

Follow most ingredients for CILANTRO-LEMON MARINADE, but substitute our Provençal herb blend for the cilantro, 1 t red wine or balsamic vinegar for the citrus juice, and 3 T red wine for the white wine or beer. Use same marinating times as above.

Harrira Stew

Here's a favorite recipe for stewing chicken. We love the simplicity of it, and we usually have everything in the pantry so we can make it on a whim. Serve with raisin cous cous. (serves 4)

1 stewing chicken cut into 8 pieces (2 legs, 2 thighs, each breasts split in half, with the wing attached)

1 onion, chopped

2 cloves garlic, chopped

3 tomatoes, diced, or 10 oz. canned tomatoes

2 1/2 pts. chicken stock or broth

1/2 tsp. cinnamon

1/2 tsp. ground ginger

1/2 tsp. ground cumin

8 oz. canned chick peas

chopped cilantro

red chili flakes or harissa (opt)

Put chicken, onion, garlic, and stock in a large pot. Bring to a boil over high heat. Skim scum. Add spices, tomatoes and chick peas. Reduce heat to simmer, and continue cooking until chicken is done, approximately 1 ½ hours. Garnish with cilantro and red chili flakes or harissa.

Raisin Cous Cous

2 cups cous cous

2 1/4 cup water or chicken broth

1 tsp. salt

1 shallot, chopped

1/3 cup raisins

1. Put raisins, shallots, water and salt in a pot. Bring to a boil. Pour in cous-cous. Stir to mix and cover the pot. Remove pot from heat, let stand for 5 minutes. Fluff cous cous with a fork.

Harissa

2 tsp. chili flakes
3 tbs. olive oil
1 clove garlic, chopped
2 tsp. ground cumin.

Put everything in a pan. Heat over low heat for about 5 minutes, or until garlic starts to brown. Remove from heat immediately so the garlic does not burn.

THE BASIC BOILED STEWING CHICKEN

We keep our hens an average of 3 years, way past the 7-week lifespan of a supermarket fryer, and so ours have real muscle development. The meat is very tender and very succulent if --and maybe only if— simmered a long time. Do not plan a same-day meal around one of these stewers: always cook it the day before, or on a day when you can start it in the morning and eat it at leisure. Average simmer times are 2 ¼ to as long as five hours. You will be well rewarded for your patience and willingness to forego a normal cooking schedule.

Free-range chickens can make wonderful stews. What follows covers the details for young free-range fryers or roasters – the most common sizes sold at supermarkets and included with your CSA subscription. Old stew chickens – the chickens from our farm -- will have better flavor, but take hours to tenderize.

Into a medium-large pot place bird, 2 teaspoon salt and enough water to barely cover. Bring to a simmer or gentle boil, cover, and cook patiently. Test for the meat just slipping off the bones beginning at 40 minutes (or 1 ½ hours if using our old hens) and at least every 10 minutes thereafter. Once meat does slip from bones, carefully lift bird out of pot with tongs, a slotted spoon, or a carving fork. Let cool. Meanwhile, strain the broth into another pot. This broth is liquid gold for happy diners as well as for flu sufferers. Remove meat from the bird and discard the bones and gristle.

You now have 2 outstanding products: the broth and the meat. Here are your options:

- use meat and broth separately, the meat for chicken salad or pasta sauces or whatever and the broth as a base for outstanding soups or gravies. The broth you've made is stellar and can be frozen nicely, without meat, greens, or pasta, for a reserve meal for sick people. Hesitant appetites can perk up really well with the cleanness of free-range flavor.

- or prepare the broth and the meat together for wonderful soups or stews. We here offer two superb simple winter soups, designed to warm you on the coldest days or to nourish sick folks.

Chicken, Garlic, And Greens Soup

Chop cooked chicken meat coarsely and return to the broth. Taste for salt and pepper. Sauté (in separate pan) 4 cloves chopped garlic in 1 T olive oil until just soft. Add all this to the broth and meat. Add also and optionally ¼ cup white wine, 1 tablespoon fresh chopped herbs, and/or small pieces of carrot, onion, and/or parsnip. Bring to a simmer.

In a second pot, cook (al dente) capellini, tortellini, macaroni, or orzo, drain, and wash with cold water.

Now assemble the 3 key ingredients: the broth and chicken, at this point fully seasoned and simmering; the pasta; and the greens. Into one large or individual serving bowls, place coarsely chopped, raw stir-fry blend, tender collards or kale, mixed mustards, or Italianate wilting mix. One to two cups raw chopped greens per person is good for a start. Add to serving bowl(s) about ¼ cup (per person) of the cooked pasta. Ladle the piping hot broth over this and gently stir for a few seconds.

Eat and enjoy. This is great served with crusty bread and a not-too-chilled Pinot Grigio or similar white wine, or with garlic bread and beer. Related variants include a chicken and greens risotto and a greens soup made not with our stewing birds but with day-after-Thanksgiving turkey, as well as the meatless greens-and-garlic soup covered earlier.

Chicken And Boiled Vegetables

As per above, coarsely chop the chicken and return it to the broth. Now add:

3 peeled carrots, cut into large 1″ pieces

3 medium or 5 small potatoes, cubed into large chunks

1 c whole baby turnips or rutabagas, or medium ones cut up, washed but not peeled

1 onion, coarsely chopped

2 c either cabbage wedges or (to be added much later) our tender greens

3 bay leaves or a pinch of fresh thyme or rosemary leaves

s and p to taste

Simmer until all vegetables are barely soft. If you opted for greens, stir them in at this point. Serve in the broth or not, and have plenty of salt and pepper ready for each diner to season their own. This is akin to the "corned beef and cabbage" group of meals, and is simple, honest, and really good.

How To Roast The Perfect Chicken Or Turkey

Courtesy of my mother, Roberta Jenkins, of Providence, RI. She is a wonderful cook and inspiration.

The recipe that follows assumes about a 22 lb. turkey, enough to feed 8-12 with some leftovers. If using a free-range chicken, use a young roaster or fryer, NOT a stew chicken. Then, reduce the seasonings proportionally, and the total cooking time to only 50 – 80 minutes.

Rub inside and out of bird with 1 ½ tablespoons of Kosher or sea salt, plus 1 ½ teaspoons of black pepper. Also rub in mixed herbs: dried or fresh minced rosemary, thyme, marjoram, and sage (2 teaspoons total of dried herbs, 2 tablespoons total of fresh, minced herbs). May include fresh parsley too.

Stuff the bird with any good stuffing.

Pre-heat oven to 375°F, and place oven rack at lowest level. Carefully open a large paper shopping bag along its seams. Oil this on both sides with a total of 3 tablespoons corn or olive oil. Tuck this in around the turkey so that the paper edges are weighted down by the bird, effectively tenting the now-covered turkey. This is the single most important step, especially for young free-range poultry. It keeps lean birds moist and performs much better than foil.

If you've bought a fresh local bird, you'll need to add about 2 cups water, white wine, or beer to the pan, and maintain about that level throughout the baking process. If the bird is free-ranged, as ours always are, it is probably lean and you should add about 3 T olive oil to the top of the bird (before tenting) or to the pan itself (after tenting).

Commercial store-bought turkeys are usually injected with water, salt, margarine, and/or butter, for which you are charged as part of the weight of the "bird". They consequently are more fatty and more watery than local birds, and so, for a commercial bird, you should reduce your water additions to a single cup initially.

Put bird in 375°Foven and bake for 45 minutes, then lower temperature to 350°F and continue baking for 1 ½ more hours. Remove and discard tent (this will let the juicy bird now brown) and continue baking until the bird's knee and hips joints feel loose if you wobble them. For bigger birds, continue cooking until the "wobble point". Total cooking times are about 2 ¾ hours for small birds and can be up to 4 hours for really big ones. Be patient and have little snacks available. The meal being perfect is more important than the clock.

Remove from oven and let sit at least 12 minutes before carving.

Recipe Index

CPSIA information can be obtained at www.ICGtesting.com
Printed in the USA
LVOW121554080312

272224LV00012B/118/P

9 781456 422806